THE ALL-NEW
SPEEDER'S GUIDE
TO AVOIDING TICKETS

A speeding ticket isn't a verdict.

It's an opening offer.

— and this book is about negotiating the hell out of it.

Kerry Lutz

America's Top Recovering Attorney/ Alleged Habitual Speeder

WARNING CITATION

YOU ARE HEREBY OFFICALLY WARNED OF THE BELOW DESCRIBED VIOLATION.
YOUR ONLY REQUIRED ACTION IS TO EXERCISE SAFER DRIVING HABITS IN THE FUTURE.

PALM BEACH GARDENS POLICE DEPARTMENT

COUNTY OF: PALM BEACH	W131304
CITY (IF APPLICABLE): PALM BEACH GARDENS	

DAY OF WEEK	MONTH	DAY	YEAR	☐ A.M. ☒ P.M.
TUESDAY	09	01	2026	02:09 P.M.

NAME (PRINT) FIRST	MIDDLE	LAST
KERRY	HAL	LUTZ

STREET: [redacted] IF DIFFERENT THAN ONE ON DRIVER LICENSE "X" HERE ▶

CITY	STATE	ZIP CODE
[redacted]	FL	[redacted]

TELEPHONE NUMBER	DATE OF BIRTH	RACE	SEX	HGT
	[redacted]	W	M	602

DRIVER LICENSE NUMBER: [redacted]

STATE	CLASS	CDL LICENSE	YR LICENSE EXP.	IF COMMERCIAL MTR. VEH. "X" HERE
FL	E	Y (N)	2029	▶ ☐

YR. VEHICLE	MAKE	STYLE	COLOR	IF PLACARDED HAZARDOUS MATERIAL "X" HERE
2024	TESL	4D	RED	▶ ☐

VEHICLE LICENSE NO.	TRAILER TAG NO.	STATE	YEAR TAG EXPIRES	IF COMPANION CITATION(S) "X" HERE
[redacted]		FL	2027	▶ ☐

UPON A PUBLIC STREET OR HIGHWAY, OR OTHER LOCATION, NAMELY

PALM BEACH GARDENS

VIOLATIONS

☐ UNLAWFUL SPEED ______ MPH SPEED APPLICABLE ______ MPH

☐ CARELESS DRIVING ☐ SAFETY BELT VIOLATION ☐ NO PROOF OF INSURANCE

☐ VIOLATION OF TRAFFIC CONTROL DEVICE ☐ IMPROPER OR UNSAFE EQUIPMENT ☐ EXPIRED DRIVER LICENSE

☐ VIOLATION OF RIGHT-OF-WAY ☐ EXPIRED TAG ☐ FOUR (4) MONTHS OR LESS

☐ IMPROPER CHANGE OF LANE OR COURSE ☐ SIX (6) MONTHS OR LESS ☐ MORE THAN FOUR (4) MONTHS

☐ IMPROPER PASSING ☐ MORE THAN SIX (6) MONTHS ☐ NO VALID DRIVER LICENSE

☐ CHILD RESTRAINT ☐ IMPROPER OR NO SIGNAL ☐ PEDESTRIAN VIOLATION

☐ IMPROPER PARKING ☐ IMPROPER TURN ☐ DRIVING TOO SLOWLY

☐ BICYCLE VIOLATION ☐ DRIVING WITHOUT LIGHTS ☐ OPEN CONTAINER

☐ OTHER:

COMMENTS PERTAINING TO VIOLATION:

[redacted]

RANK - SIGNATURE OF OFFICER | BADGE NO. | ID NO. | TROOP UNIT

WARNING CITATION

Real-Life Introduction to the D-A-M-N System

A Picture Is Worth 12 Points

I wrote The All-New Speeder's Guide to Avoiding Tickets to explain something I learned over more than fifty years behind the wheel: a speeding ticket isn't necessarily the final word. It's an opening offer. And the most valuable negotiation may take place before the officer ever puts pen to paper.

Then, on September 1, 2026, the Palm Beach Gardens Police Department gave me a chance to put my own system to the test. I was stopped and received a written warning instead of a citation. The book was already in print. Naturally, life decided to supply a new opening chapter.

I have the written warning to prove it. It is the real-life example behind this introduction, not a hypothetical courtroom victory or a story improved over a few drinks. A picture really can be worth 12 points.

The D-A-M-N System

D — De-escalate. Make the cop or trooper feel safe. His first priority is getting home after his shift. Pull over promptly, keep your hands visible, and don't make him wonder what you're doing.

A — Admit. Acknowledge the situation without jumping out and yelling, 'I did it! I did it!' Don't volunteer a precise confession, invent a story, or pick a roadside argument.

M — Mitigate. Give the officer a truthful reason to exercise discretion. Ask respectfully for a warning or, if appropriate, a reduced, non-point citation. Think of it as negotiating a plea bargain at the curb.

N — NOW! Don't wait for traffic court, a fine, or an insurance surcharge. Your best opportunity to influence the outcome may be right there at the window, before the ticket exists.

A reader named Dan from Long Island helped me see that the old three-letter name didn't capture the urgency. He was right. His suggestion meant more rewriting for me, but it gave readers something they can remember under pressure: D-A-M-N.

The next time you're stopped by a cop or state trooper, before you get angry, lose your cool, or go off on him, remember to use the D-A-M-N System.

Don't Fight the Cop. DAMN the Ticket!

Dedication

For James M. Eagan,

The trooper who turned the radar gun around, looked at it from the other side, and told the rest of us the truth.

He blazed the trail. The rest of us are just driving it — at a reasonable and prudent speed under the circumstances.

For Scotty Kilmer

Who has spent a lifetime telling the truth about the road, the machine, and the people behind the wheel. You've kept drivers honest, informed, and just a little bit safer and much wiser for the wear.

Before We Pull Out of the Driveway

Three things are certain in this life: death, taxes, and the officer at your window not caring about either. This book won't help you with the first two. It might help you with the third.

Quick housekeeping before we go. I'm a recovering attorney, not your attorney. Nothing in this book is legal advice and reading it doesn't make me your lawyer. Traffic law is different in all fifty states — sometimes different in the next county over — and it changes constantly. Before you bet anything important on a page in here, check it against the rules where you actually drive. And if the stakes are real, hire a real lawyer in your own backyard.

Second thing, and I mean this one. Nothing in this book is a license to drive like a lunatic. The best ticket-avoidance tool ever invented is the gas pedal you don't push. Everything here assumes you're a basically responsible human who occasionally drifts over the line and doesn't want one dumb afternoon to cost a license, a job, or a decade of insurance pain. Speed kills people — yours and somebody else's kids included — and no chapter in this book is worth a funeral.

Read it in that spirit and we're going to get along just fine. Now buckle up and make sure your airbag is fully charged. We are going on a journey.

Contents

PART I
FIRESTARTER NAT

Firestarter Nat

A Prologue

Long before I became a habitual speeder, there was my father Firestarter Nat. Nat Lutz belonged to a generation that saw things most of us can barely imagine. Before he entered the Army Air Corps, he was tearing up the asphalt in New Jersey. He loved speed. Once he got a speeding ticket for riding a horse over the limit. During World War II, he flew The Hump — the ultra-hazardous air route over the Himalayas between India and China. The Hump wasn't just another military assignment. It was the most dangerous air route in the world.

Pilots flew overloaded aircraft through mountain passes, violent storms, icing conditions, and primitive navigation systems across some of the most unforgiving terrain on Earth. The weather killed crews. The mountains killed crews. Navigation mistakes killed crews. Sometimes the Japanese helped. The pilots called the scattered wreckage *the Aluminum Trail.*

My father survived. I sometimes wonder whether that experience permanently altered his relationship with risk and speed. After you've spent your youth flying through the Himalayas in wartime, a speed limit sign on the New Jersey Turnpike probably seemed quite insignificant.

When the war ended, Nat came home, got married, raised a family, built houses, started businesses, paid taxes, and became a productive citizen. He also mastered the art of being a habitual speeder. Not a reckless speeder. A disciplined speeder. He had a code. He drove at a speed that he believed was appropriate under the circumstances, never mind that it was 20-40 miles faster than any other car on the road.

He never sped through residential neighborhoods and neither do I. Kids, bicycles, dogs, blind driveways, and school zones were different. Those roads demanded respect. The speed lived on highways, turnpikes, parkways, and commercial corridors. That was the code.

Nat was a super speeder before anybody knew the term existed. He purchased a 1965 Chevy Impala, his first car with factory air. He despised it. The air was fine, but every time he buried the speedometer needle (exceeded 120 miles per hour), the odometer cable snapped, rendering the gauges useless. Odometer cable replacement became routine maintenance.

Family legend also holds that after having been clocked at triple digits by a Georgia State Trooper approaching the Florida border, rather than pull over, he sped up and disappeared into an orange juice stand just over the border. As he sipped his OJ, he watched as several minutes later with lights flashing the trooper passed him by.

I wasn't there and the historical record is incomplete. And some stories do improve with age. But anybody who knew Nat never questioned that it happened.

Besides his family, flying was his true love. When traveling by air, he would study the route maps carefully tracing the takeoff and the travel route. He knew the Newark Airport runway layout by heart. On one flight into JFK, he caught the pilot making a wrong turn while taxiing. The mistake tied up airport traffic and generated a memorable discussion with air traffic control. While the other passengers were wondering which baggage carousel their luggage would arrive at, my father was tracking ground operations from seat 23A.

That's how his mind worked. He also had a unique method for determining when it was time for an eye examination. Most people realize they need glasses when they can't read a menu. Not so with Nat. For him it was time for new glasses when he stopped spotting radar traps a mile away.

"Guess I need an eye exam." "I'm having trouble making out the radar traps." As far as he was concerned, visual acuity was measured by the distance at which it took to identify a state trooper. Remarkably in all those years he drove, he had only one accident. He wasn't speeding. He wasn't racing. He wasn't outrunning anybody. He was lighting a cigarette and took his eyes off the road for a few seconds to strike a match and drove into the back of a car stopped at a toll booth.

Afterward, he announced he had discovered the true purpose of the cigarette lighter. It wasn't a convenience feature. It was a safety device. From that day forward, he only used the car lighter.

Years later he was building houses in Union and Warren Counties, New Jersey. That meant driving the infamous Route 22. Be thankful, if you've never driven the *Double-Deuce.* It's less a highway than a transportation experiment run amok. Traffic enters from every conceivable direction, stores in the median, shopping centers, delivery trucks. There are impatient commuters making questionable lane changes with everyone competing for the same piece of pavement simultaneously.

After he began making those trips, he dramatically upped his life insurance coverage. He claimed it was prudent financial planning. The rest of the family suspected he had simply developed a realistic risk assessment of Route 22. Having driven it many times myself, I could see why.

He would have loved today's technology. Modern app-enabled radar detectors would have given him an immediate unfair advantage. Waze would've blown his mind. He couldn't conceive of world where a driver five miles ahead could spot a trooper and instantly warn thousands of others.

Tesla would have fascinated him. A car that drives itself, reads speed limit signs, avoids collisions, and routes around traffic in real time? It's superior to the primitive autopilot he used while flying B24's. He would've mastered it before most people found the settings menu. Then he'd start an informal school teaching its proper use to his friends.

Looking back, I don't think my father's driving was totally about speed. I think it was about awareness, control and dopamine. He wanted to know what was ahead, where the hazards were and where the traffic was. And most importantly where the troopers were hiding. And the high that comes from outsmarting them all while traveling at triple digits never wore thin.

He flew airplanes the same way he drove cars and lived life — with his eyes open and his head on a swivel. *The road never scared him. The sky had already tried.*

This book didn't start with me. It started with a Hump pilot who survived. He buried the speedometer needle whenever circumstances permitted, and taught me that driving is about awareness, not just speed. And if there is a patron saint of habitual speeders, I know exactly who it is. **Firestarter Nat.**

PART II
HOW THEY HUNT

It's Not a Verdict. It's an Opening Offer.

For years I've repeated a line told to me by a close friend— a former criminal defense attorney who spent decades successfully fighting in the trenches of New York City's criminal courts. We were talking about the system and how bad it is. I was bitching about a speeding ticket I got on the FDR Drive in Manhattan and how when I went to the hearing, I didn't have a chance, it was open and shut. He looked up at me and said: "Kerry, it's easier to beat a murder rap in New York City than a speeding ticket."

He wasn't exaggerating. After more than 50 years of driving, 35 years since reading Eagan's book and over 100 traffic stops, roughly twenty-five speeding tickets, and countless hours spent in traffic courts from upstate New York to Palm Beach County Florida, I've learned exactly what he meant.

In a criminal case, everybody understands they're dealing with something serious. The defendant has a lawyer. The prosecutor prepares. The judge pays attention. The system, for all its flaws, knows it's making a consequential decision.

In traffic court, you're fighting a different fight. The officer/trooper in uniform is armed with his notes. He's got the radar gun and the certified calibrations records (maybe). The judge has a docket with two hundred names on it. The average unrepresented driver walks in completely clueless, assuming that because he's innocent — or close enough — that justice will somehow prevail. That's called losing before the judge bangs the gavel.

Here's a statistic that might impress you. In fourteen years of living in Florida, I've been stopped for speeding exactly seven times. I received five warnings and two tickets, and both tickets ended in conditional discharges. Zero points. Zero insurance surcharge disaster.

That's not luck. Luck doesn't run better than seventy percent in your favor for fourteen straight years across a hundred-plus lifetime stops. That's a system. And by the time you finish this book, it will be your system too.

A speeding ticket is the government's way of reminding you that physics and taxation are closely related, with a dash of safety thrown in to justify it all. You created the physics problem by pressing the pedal. The government is about to tax you for it. But here's the thing about taxes — people who understand the system pay a lot less of them than people who don't.

This is the single most important sentence I can give you: A speeding ticket isn't a verdict. It's the opening offer delivered by an armed agent in Raybans.

Most people treat that little slip of paper like the gavel already came down. Guilty. Pay up. Eat the points. Watch the insurance bill climb for five years. They sign it, they mail the check, and they never once realize they were involved in a serious negotiation and failed to make a single counteroffer.

That's right, a traffic stop and the process that follows is all a negotiation, but only if you follow the steps outlined here. How would you handle any other negotiation? A car salesman tells you a car's sticker price. Do you just say, "sounds good" and hand over the money? Of course not. You know the first number is the start of the conversation, not the end (unless you're buying a Tesla).

A ticket is exactly the same. The cop at your window is not a judge. He is the first link in a long, bored, overworked chain. And every actor that follows him wants a reason to make your file disappear, most importantly with the least amount of effort possible, usually with zero concern for the outcome. While you may be gravely offended by being singled out of a group of speeders, the system couldn't care less about you. Your ticket means nothing to the cop and nothing the judge or anyone else in the system. You are just a data point.

The officer isn't your enemy. He's just the guy whose job it was to present you state's opening offer. Your job, from the second those lights come on, is to give him a reason to reduce it or even tear it up, in other words discard the offer.

James Eagan wrote the original *bible* on this from driver's seat of a police cruiser — a retired New York state trooper who'd run the radar himself and issued thousands of tickets over the course of his career. This is the modern sequel, written by someone who studied the system and applied Eagan's methods for 35 years and achieved remarkable results. Starting there I developed many of my own techniques that fit perfectly with Trooper Eagan's.

One rule above all others, and it will repeat through this whole book: one fight at a time. Find the single spot where you've got leverage and push only there. Lawyers win by subtraction. They don't try to overturn the entire traffic enforcement system alleging that it's unconstitutional (even if we all suspect that might be the case).

How They Actually Catch You

To beat the machine you must understand how it works. Let's pop the hood and examine it before we talk about how to survive what's lurking beneath the surface. Police speed enforcement runs on three families of technology, and they behave completely differently. Knowing which one is pointed at you tells you how much warning you're going to get.

Radar — the old workhorse

Radar bounces a radio wave off your car and measures how the wave comes back. Speed shifts the frequency — that's the Doppler effect — and the gun does the math. It runs in bands. X-band is ancient and nearly extinct in real police use, though automatic supermarket doors still fire it, which is why a cheap detector screams in every grocery-store parking lot in America. K-band and especially Ka-band are the modern workhorses. Ka is the one you'll meet on the highway, and the one worth respecting.

The concept that matters: instant-on. Old radar ran continuously, which meant your detector caught the beam long before the cruiser caught you. Those days are gone. Modern radar sits silent, and the officer triggers it for a fraction of a second when he's already picked a target by eye. By the time the beam fires, you're already clocked. Your detector screaming tells you that the car ahead of you just got nailed. Useful as a herd warning. Useless as a personal shield.

Laser — the sniper

Laser otherwise known as Lidar is a different animal, and the one to genuinely respect. Instead of a wide radio cone, it fires a pencil-thin beam of infrared light — usually at your front plate from a few hundred yards. That beam targets one car, by itself, with zero ambiguity. And because it's light, your radar detector gives you essentially no advance warning. By the time it chirps, your number is already on his screen. Against a competent laser operator, your dashboard electronics are expensive decoration.

Cameras — the ones that don't care about your personality

Fixed photo-radar, speed cameras, red-light cameras, and average-speed systems that time you between two points and bill you later. No window. No charm. The ticket arrives in your mailbox weeks later with a photo of your own car attached, like a ransom note you wrote yourself. However, in Florida and around the country they are under attack. Just recently, a Broward County judge ruled that red light cameras are unconstitutional. The case will be appealed. But there's something very un-American about automated enforcement.

The bottom line: the technology decides the strategy. Against old radar, electronics buy you time. Against instant-on, they buy you a herd warning. Against laser and cameras, they buy you almost nothing. The radar gun doesn't care about your insurance rates. That's your job, so read what follows carefully.

If you're finding this book helpful, please take a moment to leave a review wherever you purchased it. Every review helps other drivers discover these strategies before their next stop — and for some of them, their license and insurance premiums may be hanging in the balance. A few words from you could save someone thousands.

Don't Be the Fish That Bites

If technology won't save you, position will. An officer working a stretch of road isn't measuring everybody. He's picking one target out of the flow. Your whole game is to never be the most interesting target in his field of view. This doesn’t mean staying at or under the limit — it's about understanding how the fish gets hooked and refusing to be the one that bites the lure.

Live in the middle of the pack

Traffic naturally clumps into loose packs. The driver who gets pulled over is almost always in the same position: he’s out front leading the pack. The leader is the guy who was flexing his macho attitude and broke away from the herd. He is now sitting alone out there, gift-wrapped, practically wearing a sign. In certain cases, the straggler at the back gets hooked, but he’s not the goal, he’s the consolation prize. The guy holding up the back may catch the cop’s attention because he’s easy prey and requires less effort to snare. It makes zero difference to anybody why you were chosen for the honor.

I suggest settling into the middle third of a group all moving the same speed so that you're just one of the crowd, of little interest to the law. If the officer wants a number today, he takes the leader or the straggler. Not the car buried in the middle.

The golden corollary, and it costs nothing to follow: never pass the pack. The single most expensive thing you can do on a highway is to be the one car obviously moving faster than everyone around you. Relative motion catches the eye and the gun. Match the flow. Don't beat it.

Use big vehicles as cover

Radar and laser both need a clean line to your vehicle. A big vehicle ahead of you — a box truck, an RV, an eighteen-wheeler — sits in that line. Tuck in a safe distance behind one and two things happen: you're harder to acquire cleanly, and the conspicuous large vehicle runs interference for you. Truckers are always searching for speed traps; their livelihood depends upon keeping a clean record. Always borrow their awareness, at a safe following distance. It's free intelligence.

A hard line: blocking never means tailgating. A big rig at a sane gap is a screen. A big rig two feet off your bumper is a casket. If the only way to use a tactic is to drive dangerously, the tactic is off the table. In high-risk driving, there are no winners.

Your Vehicle Has a Reputation

The fish-that-bites principle applies to the car itself, not just where you position it in traffic. The vehicle you're sitting in sends a signal to every officer on every road before you've touched the pedal.

My ex-wife used to drive a minivan through New York at eighty miles an hour. Never got stopped. Not once. Think about why.

Whether he knows it or not, an officer watching traffic is running a pattern-matching algorithm in his head,. He's looking for the threat profile — the muscle car, the tuned import, the sports car that looks like it's an effort to stay under 100. The minivan doesn't fit that profile. His brain files it under "obviously not a speeder" and moves on. She was doing eighty in a vehicle that registered as invisible.

That is cognitive dissonance in action. The vehicle didn't match the behavior in his mental model, so the behavior got filtered out before he ever consciously processed it. Now consider the other end of the spectrum.

A bright orange Dodge Demon — an 808- horsepower factory muscle car designed to run the quarter mile in under ten seconds — has such a firmly established reputation in law enforcement's pattern recognition that a cop should give it a ticket when it's sitting at the curb. That's not a joke. That's how deeply vehicle profile affects threat assessment. The Demon, the Hellcat, the Lambo or Ferrari with the body kit and the aftermarket exhaust — these cars announce their intentions before the ignition turns over. Every officer who sees one already knows what it was born to do.

You are not invisible. You are the opposite of invisible.

The strategic application: if you are going to drive at speeds above the tolerance threshold, the vehicle matters. The invisible car isn't always the slowest one. It's the one that doesn't register as a threat profile. A family sedan, a practical SUV, a minivan — these vehicles are cognitively filtered out in a way that a performance car never will be.

If you choose to drive the Demon, that's your right and it's a magnificent machine. But understand that you have accepted a higher level of scrutiny with every mile. You are driving a car that the officer's pattern recognition system has pre-categorized before you've done a single thing wrong. The car itself is already lining up the opening offer on your behalf.

Drive accordingly.

Read the road like it's after you

- Traps cluster at predictable spots: the bottom of long downhills, right past the sign where the limit drops at a town line, just past an off-ramp, behind overpasses and billboards. Be at the limit in those places specifically. Cuts in the median aren't just designed for troopers to cross over; they are loitering points for them to pick off unknowing speeders. Be particularly aware of the trooper on the other side of the median parked and watching on coming traffic. You're just a U-turn away from a ticket.
- Watch for the sea of brake lights. The normie unaware driver instinctively hits his brakes when he sees a cop, even if he's not speeding.

- Be aware when traffic is moving slower than normal during light traffic there could easily be a cop hiding in the right lane in front of a truck.
- Mirror discipline. Half of avoiding a stop is seeing the cruiser before it pulls out. Scan on a rhythm.

Know What You're Looking At

Radar awareness is only half the equation. The other half is knowing what the cruiser looks like before the lights come on — because by the time they do, it's too late.

Spotting a police vehicle early is a skill, and like any skill it gets better with practice. It also requires knowing what you're looking for, because the vehicle itself has changed several times over the past forty years.

The Chevy Caprice. The police car of the 1980s and into the early nineties. A generation of drivers learned to clock those distinctive taillights— the boxy silhouette, the dog-dish hubcaps, the spotlight on the driver's A-pillar. When you saw a Caprice, you paid attention, because almost any Caprice on the road was potentially a cop.

The Ford Crown Victoria Police Interceptor. The Caprice's replacement, and arguably the most iconic law enforcement vehicle in American history. The Crown Vic dominated for nearly two decades, from the mid-nineties until Ford stopped production in 2011. It became so synonymous with police work that any

Crown Vic on the road warranted a second look. The tell: the rear light cluster, the push bumper, the spotlight, and those steel wheels with the plain hubcaps that no civilian Crown Vic owner in his right mind would choose.

The Dodge Charger. The dominant police sedan today, and the one that gives itself away most dramatically at night. That distinctive LED light bar across the rear end — what I call the distributive light bar — is unmistakable. Even when the cruiser isn't running lights, that rear-end LED array has a faint glow that reads clearly from a quarter mile back in the dark. In daylight, look for the push bumper, the stripped-down trim, the spotlight, and the plain steel wheels or simple hubcaps where a civilian Charger would have alloy.

The Ford Police Interceptor Utility. The Explorer-based platform that has become increasingly common, particularly for highway patrol and suburban departments. The Expedition shows up too, to a lesser degree. Same tells as the Charger — plain wheels, push bumper, antenna clusters on the roof, the spotlight on the A-pillar, low-profile light bar nearly flush with the roofline.

The pattern across all of them: police vehicles are almost always the stripped-down model. No chrome. No fancy wheels. No exterior options. Hubcaps or basic steel wheels where any civilian owner would have spent the extra money on alloys. The fleet manager's job is durability and cost, not aesthetics, and it shows. A spotlessly maintained car with plain steel wheels and a spotlight on the A-pillar deserves your attention regardless of what model it is.

Day Tells — What's Missing and What's Added

Police vehicles are often easier to spot by what they're missing than by what they have. Every consumer trim level adds features. The fleet manager strips them out. Learn to read absence as much as presence.

Roof rails and crossbars. This is the single clearest day tell on a police SUV. A civilian Ford Explorer, Chevrolet Tahoe, or Dodge Durango almost always comes equipped with roof rails or crossbars. The police package version doesn't. The roof is either clean or carries hardware that isn't rails — antenna mounts, a low-profile light bar housing, communications equipment. Once you know to look for it, a roofline without rails but with utility hardware is an immediate flag.

Running boards. Civilian SUVs commonly have running boards or step rails along the rocker panels. Police vehicles typically don't — they're a maintenance item and can interfere with rapid door opening during stops. The clean rocker panel is a tell.

Alloy wheels. As covered: steel wheels or basic painted units where any civilian buyer would have ordered alloys. This applies to both sedans and SUVs. If the wheel looks like something ordered by a fleet manager for durability at lowest cost, it was.

Chrome and trim packages. Gone. Police packages run blacked-out or basic — no chrome mirror caps, no chrome grille, no brightwork. The civilian version glitters. The police version doesn't. A Charger that looks oddly plain next to the ones at the dealership is worth a longer look.

Body damage. Police fleet vehicles are maintained on strict schedules and repaired quickly. A government-plated vehicle with a fresh wash, no dents, and a slightly institutional look is characteristic of fleet maintenance, not private ownership.

Night Tells — What Glows

After dark the equation flips. You're no longer looking for what's absent. You're looking for what's been added — the hardware and light signatures that civilian cars simply don't have.

The Charger rear-end LED array. The most distinctive night tell in modern fleet policing. Even with emergency lights off, the LED strip embedded in the rear end below the trunk is unique. I can spot it from over a mile back. Once you've seen it, you can't unsee it. Pay attention.

The laptop screen. Every police vehicle in active service carries a mobile data terminal — the in-car computer. At night, that screen lights up the interior with a distinctive blue-white glow that reads as law enforcement the moment you see it. A lit-up cab from an interior source, not a phone, is the tell.

Interior light patterns. Officers on patrol often run interior lighting that differs from civilian vehicles — radio units, MDT screens, partition lighting in the rear, the glow of the control console. With practice, the interior lighting signature of a working cruiser reads differently from someone checking their phone.

Pace behavior. A vehicle that is matching your speed precisely, maintaining exact following distance without closing the gap or dropping back, and doing so for more than a mile, is doing something deliberate. Civilian drivers don't pace. Back off and see what it does.

Driving like a cop. This is a biggie. Cops don't drive like ordinary people. They drive with purpose and authority. They don't meander and they usually drive faster, often much fast, than surrounding traffic, when they aren't on the hunt. Interestingly, they drive the same when they are off duty as well. It's something you have to train yourself to recognize.

The Undercover Vehicle — Funny Cars

James Eagan called them funny cars, and the name has stuck in my head for over thirty years. They are the vehicles that look like ordinary civilian cars right up until the moment they don't — the unmarked, the low-profile, the deliberately nondescript.

Today's undercover setup typically reveals itself through lights. What you're looking for: a low-profile light bar sitting nearly flush with the roofline, often only visible if you know to look for it. LED strips or strobe units mounted inside the rear window, embedded behind the glass rather than on top of the car. A light package in the front grille — blue and red alternating LEDs tucked into the headlight housing or behind the grille, invisible until they activate. Inside, the glow of a laptop screen mounted to the dash.

By day the tells are subtler: plain steel wheels on a car that should have alloys, the spotlight on the A-pillar, antenna clusters that don't belong on a civilian model, a push bumper or reinforced front end. The car that seems to be pacing you — matching your speed without visibly driving to a destination — is worth noticing.

Funny cars are less common than they were in Eagan's day. Budget pressures have pushed most departments toward marked vehicles, and the liability concerns around unmarked enforcement have grown. But they still exist, particularly on state highway patrol, in speed enforcement units, and in jurisdictions that run active speed details. The experienced driver knows they're out there and factors them into his awareness, even if the odds of encountering one on any given day are lower than they used to be.

The bottom line on vehicle recognition is the same as every other principle in this chapter: awareness is the skill. The driver who knows what a Charger's rear light assembly looks like at night, who notices the plain wheels on the Interceptor two lanes over, who catches the glow of the laptop screen in the sedan that's been sitting in his mirror for the last mile — that driver gets the warning. The driver on autopilot gets the lights.

None of this is exotic. It's the difference between driving on autopilot and driving awake — which, conveniently, is also the difference between a safe driver and a dangerous one. The same habits that keep the points off your license also keep you alive. This is self-evident but many people miss it.

The Real Number — Understanding Enforcement Tolerance

The posted speed limit is the law. Let's be straight about that. One mile per hour over the number on the sign is, technically, a violation in every state that runs an absolute limit system, which is most of them.

But you and I both know the posted limit is not always the number that gets you pulled over.

That gap between the law as written and the law as enforced has a name: enforcement tolerance. It's informal, it's not guaranteed, it varies from officer to officer and jurisdiction to jurisdiction and hour to hour. But it exists and understanding how it actually operates is as useful as anything else in this book.

What Tolerance Is — and Isn't

Enforcement tolerance is not a legal right. There is no statute anywhere in the United States that says officers shall ignore drivers going fewer than ten miles per hour over the limit. No court has given you a free pass up to any particular buffer. The officer has complete discretion to write you up for one over if he chooses.

What tolerance is, is a practical reality of how enforcement operates on American roads. Officers focus time and resources on the most egregious violations. Writing every driver doing two over the limit on a busy interstate would generate paperwork without improving safety. The radar reading, the traffic context, the officer's judgment, the department's priorities — all of these feed into a decision that happens in seconds, every single time.

The result, in practice, is that most officers work within informal buffers. What those buffers look like depends on everything that follows.

The General Numbers — and Why They're Not Rules

In urban and suburban settings, enforcement attention tends to sharpen at around five miles per hour over the posted limit. On interstates and highways, ten to twelve over is where many officers begin to seriously consider a stop, though some states and jurisdictions run significantly tighter.

These are generalizations. Dangerous ones if you treat them as guarantees.

The officer who will write you at one over exists. The officer who won't bother until fifteen over exists. The same officer can make different calls on different days depending on conditions, directives from supervisors, the volume of the morning, and whether anything else is competing for his attention. Speed tolerance is not a number. It's a judgment call made fresh every single stop.

The number that matters most is not miles per hour over the limit. It's how visible you are. Visibility is exposure. Speed creates visibility, but visibility is what gets you stopped.

Zero Tolerance — Where the Buffer Disappears

Some zones operate without any informal tolerance at all and treating them like open highway is one of the most reliable ways to earn a ticket — or worse.

School zones are the obvious one. Posted limits are already reduced — often to twenty-five — and enforcement is frequently aggressive. Some states have mandatory fines that judges cannot waive or reduce. In a school zone, during school hours, the sign is the number. Period.

Construction and work zones carry doubled fines in most states by statute. The legislature has already decided that violations in work zones require extra deterrence, and they have built the consequence into law. This is not the place to test anybody's patience.

Residential neighborhoods are, for me, a matter of code — the same code Firestarter Nat observed and passed down. Kids on bikes, dogs in driveways, blind corners, people backing out of spots they've backed out of for twenty years. These roads demand a different gear entirely. Not because enforcement is necessarily heavier. Because the cost of a mistake here is different from the cost of a mistake on an open highway.

The Variables That Change Everything

Tolerance isn't a fixed number. It's a function of multiple variables that shift constantly and invisibly.

Time of day: At two in the morning on an empty road, a single car moving fifteen over the limit is conspicuous in a way it would never be in afternoon traffic. The officer has fewer targets competing for his attention. In rush hour, with hundreds of cars moving at roughly the same speed, enforcement becomes selective by necessity. The lonely car on a dark road is always the most visible thing on it.

Traffic flow: Probably the most important variable most drivers never think about explicitly. An officer watching a highway where everyone is moving at seventy-five in a seventy zone is unlikely to make a stop. An officer watching the same road where traffic is at sixty and one car is doing eighty has an obvious target. Tolerance isn't just about your speed. It's about your speed relative to everyone around you. This is the fish-that-bites principle in its purest form.

The state and jurisdiction: Western states with long straight highways and sparse populations have historically run with more practical tolerance than the northeastern corridor. Photo enforcement and speed camera states run zero tolerance at camera locations regardless of informal culture elsewhere. A small rural department with two officers has different bandwidth than a county with a dedicated speed enforcement unit. Know the territory you're driving.

The vehicle: Sports cars, heavily modified vehicles, and cars running aggressively in traffic draw more visual attention in some jurisdictions. This isn't universal and it isn't fair, but it's part of the real picture. Anything that makes you stand out increases your exposure, and the car is part of what makes you stand out.

Funny story my oldest friend Geoff was driving on the New York Thruway one time. He always had a habit of talking strangers at rest stops especially cops. One day he's talking to a trooper and just asks him outright, how fast do I have to be going to get a ticket. The trooper gave him a thoughtful look and replied, "That's for me to know and you to find out." He wasn't giving out any trade secrets to curious onlookers, but I guarantee you he had a tolerance number too.

The Speedometer Reality

Here's something most drivers don't know: factory speedometers are almost universally calibrated to read slightly fast rather than your actual speed. A reading of seventy miles per hour on most stock vehicles corresponds in real life to a speed of sixty-seven to sixty-nine.

Manufacturers do this intentionally. A speedometer that overestimates speed nudges drivers toward slightly slower speeds, which has a marginal safety benefit. And no driver complains that their speedometer makes them feel faster than they are — but plenty would complain if they got a ticket while their gauge said they were within the limit.

There's also a liability angle to this. Imagine the class actions from driver groups if they got nailed for exceeding the speed limit because their speedometer was too slow.

GPS-based speed readings, by contrast, are accurate to within a mile per hour. If you've ever noticed the gap between your speedometer and your navigation app's speed readout, that's the calibration difference in action.

This doesn't give you a legal defense, and it doesn't change the radar reading. But it's part of the real picture of how the numbers actually work in the car you're driving.

Kerry's Tolerance Rule

After fifty years of driving, my personal operating principle isn't a number of miles per hour over the limit.

It's a question I ask myself constantly:

Am I visible?

Not visible in the sense of "can someone see my car." Visible in the sense of "am I standing out from the flow around me." A car moving at the same speed as the pack, buried in the middle of the pack, with no erratic behavior and nothing unusual about it, is not visible. It's background. It could be doing fifty-five or seventy-five, and to an officer who has to pick a target, it's an unremarkable blur.

As previously stated, a car moving faster than everyone around it — or slower — or doing something odd with lane changes — or sitting right out in front where the pack used to be — that car is visible. Speed may have created the visibility, but the visibility is the actual exposure.

Drive so you're not the answer to anyone's question. That's the tolerance rule. Not a number, not a guarantee — just the practical wisdom of a long time spent watching who gets stopped and who drives home.

The Trooper Doing 65

Here's the smartest free lesson you'll ever get on a Florida highway or any other one in the United States. Picture I-95 on a weekday afternoon. Traffic's moving — and then it isn't. Up ahead, everything bunches up and slows to a crawl. A rolling wall of brake lights stretching back what feels like a mile. Nobody's passing. Nobody's weaving. Everybody's just hovering there, patient as monks, at a polite sixty-five miles an hour.

Why? Because way up at the front of that whole parade is a Florida Highway Patrol trooper. And he's doing exactly sixty-five. Every driver in that backup has figured out the same thing simultaneously, without a word to each other. As long as that trooper is out front setting the pace, sixty-five is the law, regardless of the posted number. Sixty-five, because the man with the badge decided that's today's speed limit.

So, everybody hangs back and behaves. It's beautiful, in a way. A thousand strangers, perfect cooperation, no committee meeting required. And then there's that one guy. There's always that one guy. He gets antsy. He's got somewhere to be. He decides the rules of physics and law enforcement don't apply to him today. He pulls out, swings into the left lane, and drives around the trooper.

Around the trooper! Schmuck!

You already know how this ends. The lights come on before he's even fully back in the lane. The trooper peels out of the parade and lights him up like a stadium. And the entire backed-up procession rolls past the scene, gradually picking up speed, every single driver thinking the exact same thought:

Better him than me. The lesson, and it's one of the most reliable rules in this whole book.

Never pass a moving trooper. And the deeper version: *If a trooper is driving the speed limit, so are you.* He's not doing sixty-five because his cruiser can't go faster. He's doing sixty-five because he decided to, and the second somebody blows past him that person has personally and voluntarily declared himself the fastest car on the road in full view of a law enforcement officer. You couldn't write yourself a clearer ticket if you mailed it to the courthouse with a stamp.

When you find yourself stuck behind a trooper, don't fight it. Don't fume. Settle in, match his speed, and treat it for the gift it is for the next few miles, somebody with a badge is personally guaranteeing you cannot get a speeding ticket as long as you stay behind him. If you pass him at whatever speed, he's going to view it as a sign of disrespect and make you pay for it.

Call it an escort service. The only one in this business that's actually free.

The Waze Revolution

For decades, the speeding game was a hardware arms race. They built better radar, you bought a better detector, they went instant-on, you bought a better-better detector, they went laser, you bought a laser detector that mostly chirped after you were already caught. Round and round it went. Then something changed the whole board, and it didn't come from a gadget company. It came from a map app.

Every driver ahead of you is now a scout

Crowdsourced highway intelligence — Waze, and the police-reporting features now baked into Apple Maps, Google Maps, and other mainstream apps — turned the entire driving public into one giant early-warning network. Somebody five miles ahead spots a cruiser behind a billboard and taps a button. Now it's on your map with miles to spare. A speed trap, a parked cop, a hazard — reported by a stranger you'll never meet, handed to you for free, before you ever get there.

Think about what that means. The radar detector was always reactive — it could only warn you about a beam that already existed, aimed at a car that was usually you. The map is predictive. It warns you about the parked cruiser who hasn't pointed anything at anybody yet. It handles the fixed camera, the average-speed corridor, every threat your detector is useless against.

And now the radar detector manufacturers have gotten into the act, creating app enabled detectors that passively report upcoming radar traps to their app-enabled customers.

Where it shines, where it doesn't

- Best on roads you don't know. On your daily route you already know where the cops sit. On a strange highway in a strange state, the crowd is your local knowledge, and it's remarkably good.
- Only as good as the crowd. Packed interstate at rush hour: spookily accurate. Empty back road at 2 a.m.: you're on your own.
- The one safety: mount the phone legally and don't fiddle with it while moving. A distracted-driving ticket is a real ticket with real points. Getting one while trying to avoid a speed trap is the kind of irony that hits you right in the wallet.

The modern toolkit in one sentence: an app-enabled radar detector plus Waze, run by an alert driver who's actually watching the road. The detector handles the live beam; the apps handle the threat you can't see yet. Everything beyond that trades a small fine for a big liability. The smartest device in the car is still the one holding the steering wheel.

Detectors, Jammers, and Which One to Buy

Let's settle the hardware question. There is an enormous amount of nonsense sold in this category, so let's separate what's real from what's marketing, what's legal from what will land you in far worse trouble than a speeding ticket, and — since people always ask — which detectors are actually worth the money.

What a radar detector does — and doesn't

A radar detector is a receiver. It listens for police radar bands and warns you. In most of the country, in a passenger car, perfectly legal. The exceptions: Virginia bans them in passenger vehicles, D.C. bans them, federal rules forbid them in big commercial trucks. Check your state before you mount one.

What it does: buys you reaction time against old-style radar, warns you when someone nearby just caught an instant-on burst. What it doesn't do: protect you against laser, or against photo and average-speed cameras. Treat it as a situational-awareness tool, not a force field.

Which detector, specifically

People always ask. I'll tell you what's on the market and what to look for — I won't endorse any single product, because technology moves fast and whatever was current when this was written might be obsolete by the time you read it. What doesn't change is what to look for.

Valentine One (V1): The cult classic. The V1's signature feature is directional arrows that tell you where the threat is — ahead, behind, or to the side — which no other detector quite matches. It's never been the most sensitive on raw Ka performance, but the directional intelligence makes it uniquely useful on multi-lane highways where the threat could be anywhere. Valentine has been iterating the platform for decades. If you want to know where the beam is coming from, this is the answer.

Escort (Redline 360c, MAX 360c): Escort's high-end models compete seriously on Ka sensitivity and have excellent GPS-based false-alert filtering, which means they learn to ignore the doors at your local grocery store and save their screaming for actual threats. The 360c designation means directional arrows, putting it in the same conversation as the Valentine on that front. Escort also has a mobile app ecosystem that crowdsources alerts. Good all-around package.

Uniden (R8, R7, R3): The Uniden R series became the enthusiast's value pick for good reason — raw Ka sensitivity that competes with detectors costing twice as much, solid GPS false-alert filtering, and a price point that doesn't require a second mortgage. The R8 added directional antennas. If you want the best bang-for-dollar on pure detection performance, the R series is where serious drivers start the conversation.

Cobra and budget units: They exist. For casual drivers who want something rather than nothing, they'll catch K-band and some Ka. They won't perform with the big three on sensitivity or false-alert filtering, and on the highway, false alerts are the thing that kills you — because when everything sounds like a threat, you stop believing it. Spend the money on a real unit if you're going to do this.

What to look for when you shop

- Ka-band sensitivity: where the real police radar lives. This is the spec that matters most.
- GPS-based false-alert filtering lets the unit learn your regular routes and ignore repeat non-threats. Worth every dollar.
- Low-speed muting: cuts false alerts in town, where BSM (blind-spot monitoring) from other cars sets detectors off constantly.
- App integration: crowdsourced alerts, over-the-air updates. This is where the product lives now.
- Directional display: do you want to know where the threat is? Pay for arrows.

Jammers: where I get off the bus

Laser jammers are active devices that fire back at the officer's lidar. Several states outlaw them, and the list moves around — California, Colorado, Illinois, Minnesota, Texas, Virginia and D.C. among the notable ones.

Radar jammers — devices that actively transmit to defeat police radar — are illegal everywhere in the country under federal law. They broadcast on regulated frequencies. Getting caught with one can turn a two-hundred-dollar speeding ticket into a federal problem that makes the original charge look like a parking nuisance.

Passive detectors listen. Jammers talk back. Listening is legal almost everywhere. Talking back is where the handcuffs live. The distinction matters enormously.

The $250 Ticket That Costs $2,500

I want you to do some math with me, because nobody does this math at the roadside, and not doing it is exactly how people make consistently terrible decisions about whether to fight a ticket.

Here's the story. You get a moderate speeding ticket. Let's say the fine is $250, which is not an unusual number for a 15-over in a lot of states. You look at it, you decide $250 isn't worth a morning in court, and you mail the check. Case closed. You've moved on. Except you haven't really moved on. You've just started to pay.

The actual math on a $250 ticket

Fine: $250. Add court costs and administrative fees, which vary by state but typically run another $50 to $100. Call it $325 out of pocket on day one.

But the conviction just landed on your driving record, and it's going to sit there for three to five years depending on your state and carrier. In that window, your insurer runs your record — maybe at renewal, maybe immediately — and reprices you based on what they find. A single moderate speeding conviction raises a typical premium by somewhere between 20% and 40%. If you're paying $1,500 a year for coverage, that's $300 to $600 extra per year. Over three years, that's $900 to $1,800. Over five years, up to $3,000.

Add it up: $325 on day one, plus $1,800 or more over five years, and your $250 ticket just became a $2,100-plus event. And that's the moderate version.

What the serious ticket actually costs

Push it to 25 or 30 over the limit — not unusual for a highway stop — and the numbers get uglier fast. Fines in the $400 to $600 range are common. Surcharges in some states add another layer on top of the fine. Insurance hit climbs to 40% or 50% on a serious offense. On a $2,000 annual premium, that's $800 to $1,000 extra per year, for up to five years. And if it's your second offense inside the surcharge window, the multiplication starts over on top of the existing increase.

If you want to feel real pain, try explaining to your spouse why the car insurance just went up $600 a year for a ticket you paid $300 to avoid fighting. Do the calculation. It focuses the mind wonderfully. And it's the real reason you need this book. Forget about your last ticket, we are focused on your next one.

The ROI of fighting

Now run the other side of the ledger. A traffic lawyer in most markets charges several hundred dollars for a straightforward speeding matter. Court costs if you fight and lose run roughly the same as if you'd just paid. A defensive-driving course costs an afternoon and $50 to $100 depending on the state.

Measure any of those against a $1,500 to $3,000 five-year insurance tax and the math becomes embarrassingly simple. You are not deciding whether to spend a morning in court versus paying $250. You are deciding whether to spend a morning in court versus paying $2,500 over the next five years. Change the denominator and the decision changes with it.

The operating principle: the fine is the cheapest part of a speeding conviction. The real cost is the invisible multi-year tax that starts running the moment you drop that check in the mailbox. Know the full price before you decide whether to pay it.

The hierarchy of outcomes, ranked by actual cost

1. Dismissal or warning: nothing. The only outcome that costs you zero at every level.
2. Conditional discharge or deferral: stay clean for a set period and the charge vanishes. Usually no points, no insurance hit.
3. Reduction to a non-moving violation: you pay a fine, but it typically carries no points and often never touches your insurer.
4. Traffic school in exchange for no points: costs time and a course fee. Protects the record and the premium. Underrated by everyone.

5. Plain conviction: fine plus points plus the five-year insurance tax. The outcome this whole book exists to help you avoid.

Notice that mailing the check — the path of least resistance, the one the system is built to make easy — lands you on the worst rung of the ladder. The game is refusing the easy bad outcome.

If this book helps you downgrade or eliminate one speeding ticket, that's an enormous return on investment. The techniques in this book have saved me thousands in fines, court costs and insurance escalations, not to mention a couple of suspensions and revocations.

Fifty States, Fifty Rulebooks

There's no such thing as "the speeding law." There are at least fifty of them, plus a thicket of county and city variations underneath, and the most expensive mistake a confident driver makes is assuming the rules from his last state follow him across the line.

They don't. Here's where states actually diverge — the differences that change what you do.

Absolute, presumed, and basic

- Absolute limit: the number on the sign is the law. One over is technically a violation. Most enforcement works this way.
- Presumed limit: exceeding the posted limit is presumed unsafe — but you can argue you were nonetheless driving safely for conditions. A real defense that opens a door that simply doesn't exist in absolute-limit states.
- Basic speed law: almost every state also bans driving too fast for conditions even when you're under the limit.

That's how you get a ticket doing 55 in a 65 during an ice storm.

Where the cliff is

Many states add criminal-grade penalties once you cross a threshold. Virginia is famously aggressive — speeds that wouldn't raise an eyebrow on a wide western interstate can be charged as a misdemeanor, with a record and potential jail time. Super-speeder surcharges stack in many states, such as Georgia. Know where the criminal line sits before you press the pedal.

Who lets you off the hook

- Florida lets eligible drivers elect a driver-improvement course to keep points off the record. Most residents never fully use this escape hatch.
- Many states offer traffic school credit but cap how often you can use it — once every twelve or eighteen months is typical.
- Some jurisdictions deal freely on first offenses. Others almost never do. Find out which kind of place you're standing in before you open your mouth.

The rule: before deciding how to handle any ticket, learn three things about that specific jurisdiction — absolute or presumed limit, where the criminal threshold is, and what diversion is available on a first offense. Five minutes on the state's own website answers all three, and those five minutes determine everything.

The National Driver Register — Why the Old State-Line Trick Is Dead

For decades, a certain category of driver with a badly damaged record would simply move to another state, hand over a clean out-of-state license application, and start fresh. New state, new plate, new record. That trick worked beautifully, right up until the moment it stopped working entirely.

Today every state DMV checks the National Driver Register the moment you hand over your paperwork for a new license. The NDR is a unified federal database that flags revocations, suspensions, and serious violations regardless of which state they happened in. If your old state has already processed a revocation, a red flag appears on the clerk's screen before she's finished typing your name. She hands your paperwork back and tells you to go clear your suspension in the state you came from. The state line doesn't protect you anymore.

However, knowing exactly how the system works reveals where the timing still matters.

The Pre-Conviction Window — When the State Line Still Buys You Something

Here's the move, and it requires precision. I am not encouraging you to move to another state in order to avoid a suspension or revocation. But if you were planning to move anyway, or decided that you're tired of the North's cold winters and are ready for a move south this is the way to do it. The NDR flags revocations and suspensions. It does not flag pending cases. If you are facing a pile of points that will trigger a revocation when your case is finally decided, you have a window: the period between receiving the ticket and the court's final disposition.

During that window, your license is still technically valid and clean. No revocation has been processed. No flag has been raised. If you transfer your license to a new state before the gavel drops, the new state runs the NDR check, sees a valid active license, and issues you a new one. You are now officially under their point system and their jurisdiction.

When your old state court finally convicts you months later, it reports the violation to your new home state through the Driver License Compact. Some states recalculate out-of-state violations under their own point values. An infraction that would have triggered an automatic revocation in your old state may look like an ordinary moving violation to your new state. You get points. You pay a fine. But your new license survives.

The critical checklist if you are actually navigating this scenario:

- Never blow a court date. Legitimate adjournments are fine. A Failure to Appear triggers its own suspension and a bench warrant that hits the NDR instantly. The whole strategy collapses.
- Clear your old state's fees. Even if the points don't follow you, unpaid fines can generate an administrative suspension that catches up eventually.

- Transfer the license while the case is still pending and your current license is completely valid. After the conviction, the window closes.

This is the extreme end of the playbook. Most drivers will hopefully never need it. But in a system built entirely on administrative rules and timing, knowing exactly when to exit the arena is sometimes the ultimate legal maneuver.

The Five States That Don't Share Through the Compact

The Driver License Compact currently covers 45 states and the District of Columbia. Five states are not members and do not share routine traffic violation information through the Compact: Georgia, Massachusetts, Michigan, Tennessee, and Wisconsin.

If you receive a moving violation in one of these five states and your home state is a Compact member, the reporting mechanism is weaker. The conviction may not automatically follow you home the way it would from a member state.

The critical caveat — and read this carefully: non-Compact status is not a free pass. All five states still participate in the National Driver Register, which tracks serious offenses, revocations, and suspensions. A DUI, a reckless driving charge, or a suspension in any of these states will still find you through the NDR. What non-Compact status affects is the routine point-reporting pipeline — not the serious stuff. These states may also share information through bilateral agreements or the Non-Resident Violator Compact. Check the specific rules of both the violation state and your home state before assuming anything doesn't follow you.

PART III
DAMAGE CONTROL

The Psychology of a Traffic Stop

Why Most Drivers Lose Before the Officer Reaches the Window

Most speeding tickets are not won or lost in court. They are won or lost in the first ninety seconds after the lights come on. Drivers think traffic enforcement is primarily a legal process. It isn't. It's a psychological process. The officer approaches your car with incomplete information and a decision to make — warning, ticket, reduced charge, further investigation. Your behavior in those first ninety seconds often determines which path he takes.

This chapter explains the psychology operating on both sides of the window. Understand it and you've won half the fight before you say a single word.

The Officer Has Already Formed an Opinion

Before a word is spoken, the officer is observing and assessing you. How quickly did you pull over? Did you signal? Are your hands visible? Are you digging around inside the car? Are you acting nervous, angry, or cooperative?

His first order of business is to go home after his shift. Are you a threat to his personal safety? Your first order of business is to eliminate or downgrade the potential threat. The first thing I do when I pass a cop and know that he's coming after me, is apply my turn signal while quickly and safely pulling over to the side of the road, sometimes before he even puts his cruiser into gear. Let the officer or trooper know that you are voluntarily submitting to his authority. I have actually had cops thank me for pulling over so quickly and not making them come after me.

Always remember that traffic stops are potentially high-risk, high-tension situations. Besides having to get out of his car on an active highway, the cop needs to prepare himself for a potential life and death situation. His adrenaline is flowing and he may have even unclipped his holster.

If it's nighttime or you have tinted windows, immediately turn on your dome light, lower your window and keep your hands on the wheel where he can see them. This shows him that you are compliant and respect his safety and position. Many people already have their license and registration in hand before the cop reaches their window. Huge mistake! You need to slow the situation down so you can hopefully talk your way out of the ticket.

By the time he reaches your window, his initial assessment is complete. It happened in the sixty seconds between when he hit the lights and when he knocked on your glass. You shaped that impression whether you knew it or not.

Here's the one you should write down: you don't get a second chance at a first impression. The driver who signals, pulls over promptly and completely, turns on the dome light, and puts both hands on the wheel has already told the officer something important before either of them has spoken. He's told him: this is going to be easy.

Every Officer Expects a Fight

Here's what the officer knows before he reaches your window: most drivers immediately choose one of four responses.

1. Denial. "I wasn't speeding."
2. Excuses. "My speedometer is off." "Everybody else was doing it."
3. Anger. "You should be out catching real criminals."
4. Argument. "Your radar can't be accurate."

He's heard them all, in those exact words and every variation, hundreds of times before. Each of those responses does the same thing: it creates friction. The officer becomes psychologically invested in the ticket. He's not just enforcing the law anymore — he's defending his professional judgment against someone who just challenged it. The warning option window starts closing.

The officer not only expects resistance he's ready to make you pay for it. Which means the single most powerful thing you can do is the one thing he's not prepared for. **Don't give it to him.**

It Isn't Personal — And Don't Make It So

Former Trooper James Eagan understood something about traffic enforcement that most drivers never figure out until the ticket is already in their hand.

The officer doesn't care if he gives the ticket to you or the car three lengths ahead of you. He was ready to write one. Somebody is going to get it. Until you do something to distinguish yourself — positively or negatively — you are largely interchangeable with every other driver in his field of vision. He picked your car. He could have picked another. He is not thinking about you personally. He is thinking about a number on a radar gun.

That is not cynical. That is actually the best news you will receive all day, if you understand it and use it to your advantage.

Don Miguel Ruiz, in *The Four Agreements*, gives us two pieces of wisdom that belong on every driver's dashboard right next to the radar detector: **Don't take anything personally. Don't make assumptions.**

The officer who pulled you over did not do it because he dislikes you. He does not know you. He has not thought about you. It was time for him to make a stop, and your car was the available candidate, and that's the reason you are where you are. The moment you genuinely understand that the anger that was about to detonate the next ninety seconds of your life starts to drain away.

And don't assume he has it in for you. Don't assume he is filling a quota, targeting out-of-state plates, or that the universe decided to make your Tuesday miserable. Maybe some of those things are occasionally true. But the assumption that turns a manageable stop into a catastrophe is the one that puts you on the defensive before a single word has been spoken.

Assumptions make you tense. Tension makes you difficult. Difficult makes the ticket automatic. The officer is not your enemy. He is not your judge. He is a person doing a job who is going to write a ticket to somebody today. For the next ninety seconds you have a genuine opportunity to make sure that somebody is not you.

Understand that it's not personal and act accordingly. If you don't understand this and believe that the cop has it in for you, the stop is lost before the window comes down.

The Cognitive Dissonance Effect

One day in Jupiter, Florida, a young cop pulled me over and informed me that he clocked me doing 64 in a 45 and as if that wasn't enough, I blew through three stop signs. Every other driver in my position would start arguing. Instead, I looked at him and said:

"Officer, if I was doing 64 in a 45, then you have to give me a ticket. I earned it."

The poor kid looked completely confused and dumfounded. It was like I'd broken his software. Here's what happened, psychologically: the officer expected denial. What he got was not just agreement, but support and encouragement for his actions. That's cognitive dissonance on steroids — when reality doesn't match expectation, the brain stalls and recalibrates. The script disappeared. The adversarial dynamic disappeared with it. Suddenly we were two human beings having a conversation instead of a cop and a suspect running through their respective roles.

When the expected fight doesn't happen, the officer has to decide what to do with the space it left behind. In my experience, he fills it with curiosity. He asked why I was in such a hurry. I told him I was late for a date. He asked if she was hot. I said smoking. He laughed. I drove away with no ticket.

The lesson isn't charm: it's disruption. People are more generous when their expectations are disrupted. The officer who expected a fight and didn't get one is an officer who suddenly has options he didn't have thirty seconds ago. Give him those options and let him choose the good one.

Why Lying Is Usually Stupid

This one I learned the hard way, at my own expense, with my own son on the other end of the phone. I got stopped for speeding. I was in a hurry. And instead of running the approach that's worked for me more than two-thirds of the time, I got creative. I told the trooper my son was sick.

He said: "Call him."

I figured he was bluffing. He wasn't. He took the phone out of my hand and asked my son directly if he was okay. My son, who was perfectly fine and had no idea he was testifying, said so. The trooper handed me back the phone and handed me a ticket.

The structural problem with any lie at a traffic stop is that modern officers have radios, databases, cell phones, and thirty years of experience evaluating stories. The world has gotten very small very fast, and anything that can be checked in thirty seconds probably will be.

The officer may forgive speeding. He will rarely forgive dishonesty. Dishonesty also changes the moral equation of the whole encounter. Up until the lie, you were presumably a decent person who made a small mistake. After the lie, you're a person who tried to manipulate him. Those are different files. They get treated differently. While the truth might not set you free, an uncovered lie is asking him to throw the ticket book at you.

The Human Need to Be Respected

Think about what an officer's day actually looks like. He pulls people over all day. Most of those people argue, make excuses, insult him, or perform one of the four standard routines. He deals with complaints and confrontation as a baseline professional experience.

The driver who is calm, respectful, and professional stands apart immediately. Not because the officer is looking for flattery — he isn't and laying it on thick reads as manipulation. Authentic respect is genuinely rare, which causes most cops to take notice. Most people miss this point entirely as did Firestarter Nat.

Respect is not submission. Respect is strategic and it's the right thing to do. You can be completely respectful of the officer's role while preserving all your rights. You can decline a search politely. You can refuse to answer questions beyond what's required, politely. You can be cooperative and self-possessed at the same time. In fact, the driver who is calmly respectful without being a pushover often earns more genuine regard than the one who's either combative or sycophantic. The officer is a professional doing a job. The winning move is to treat him as such.

Why Talking Too Much Kills You

I have watched drivers beat themselves in traffic stops. Not because the officer outmaneuvered them — because they simply would not stop talking. They couldn't take yes for an answer.

The first explanation is almost always the best one. Everything after that creates risk. People talk themselves into tickets. They talk themselves into searches. They talk themselves into additional charges that weren't on the table thirty seconds earlier. They fill silences with information the officer wasn't looking for and now can't ignore. The discipline is simple and almost impossible for most people. Make your point and stop talking. Silence after you've said your piece is not suspicious. It's not rude. It's the behavior of a composed person who said what needed to be said and is now waiting for the officer to do his job. Let him do it. The pause feels longer to you than it does to him. Every extra sentence is a gamble. Usually a small one, but sometimes it's the sentence that hands him the ticket he was already half-deciding not to write.

The Psychology of Mercy

Why do warnings exist? Officers aren't required to give them. They could ticket every single stop. They don't, because discretion exists — and discretion is a psychological phenomenon, as well as a legal one.

Most officers want to believe they're dealing with a decent person who just got caught. Not criminals. Not reckless lunatics. Just regular people who let the needle drift on a long straight road. That's a story an officer can tell himself, and it's a story that ends in a warning. Your job is to keep him believing it. That makes the warning easy for him to justify — to himself, to his sergeant, to anyone who might ask later why he let someone go who was doing 64 in a 45.

Caveat, always remember the officer has access to your full driving record. Your prior convictions, DWI's, criminal record, registration status and insurance status. So, before he even gets to your door, he's got an impression of you.

Don't demand or expect mercy. Create conditions where mercy feels warranted. Don't say "I don't deserve this ticket." That's a demand. Instead, give him a small human reason — a true one — and let him arrive at mercy on his own. The warning he decided to give is far more reliable than the one you tried to pressure him into.

The Easy File Theory

This is one of the most important concepts in the book, and it applies far beyond the roadside. Every person in this system is overworked. The officer has a full shift ahead. The prosecutor has a Tuesday calendar with three hundred names on it. The clerk has a stack of files that reaches the ceiling. The judge has been listening to traffic cases since eight in the morning and it's not yet ten.

In that environment, the file that is easiest to close favorably gets closed favorably. Not out of corruption — out of simple human economics. Nobody fights harder than they have to. The cooperative defendant who shows up prepared, asks politely, and makes the entire transaction painless is the one who gets the conditional discharge. The difficult file creates resistance. The easy file creates opportunities.

The entire strategy of this book — the roadside, the courtroom, the mail, the adjournments — can be compressed into four words: **Be the easy file.**

Firestarter Nat's Rule

My father, Nat Lutz, flew The Hump over the Himalayas in wartime. He survived that and came home and drove like he was still on a mission — burying the speedometer needle on every parkway and turnpike in New Jersey, spotting radar traps from a distance at which most people couldn't even see a blur.

But here's the thing about Nat that matters for this chapter: his record was actually quite good. Because what he did wasn't just speeding. It was awareness. He knew what was ahead. Where the traps were. How the road was going to behave. What the conditions meant. He processed the environment around him like the pilot he was — constantly, systematically, with his head on a swivel.

The psychology of a traffic stop begins long before the lights come on. It begins with how you drive, how you read the road, how you carry yourself when the blue lights appear in your mirror. By the time the officer reaches your window, you've either set up a warning or you've set up a ticket, and the margin between them is almost entirely a function of awareness and composure, not speed and luck.

The rule, the one underneath all the rest: Once the officer reaches your window, the ticket is no longer about speed. It's about people. And people, given half a reason, tend toward kindness. Give him half a reason and you might just be surprised by the results.

The Stop — De-escalate, Admit, Mitigate, NOW!

The lights are on behind you. Everything in the first half of this book just failed. Good news: you've arrived at the highest-leverage ninety seconds of the entire process. The officer walking up to your window may still be deciding between a warning and a ticket. My method is the D-A-M-N System: De-escalate, Admit, Mitigate, NOW! In that order.

Before he reaches the window

I am repeating these words because they are essential. Your stop starts the second you see the lights. Signal, slow down, pull fully onto the shoulder — promptly, not dramatically. At night, flip the dome light on. Roll the window down. Hands at the top of the wheel where he can see them. Don't go digging through the glovebox while he's approaching — a hand disappearing into a dark compartment is how a routine stop goes sideways.

Everything you do in those few seconds tells the officer, before a word is spoken, whether his afternoon is about to be easy or hard. Easy is what you're selling.

De-escalate — Make the Officer Feel Safe

First, de-escalate. The officer's immediate concern is whether this stop will end safely and whether he'll go home after his shift. Signal, pull over promptly, keep your hands visible, and avoid sudden movements. A calm, predictable driver gives him one less thing to worry about.

Understand what the roadside moment is actually for: it's an opportunity to entirely avoid the ticket. Not for building a defense. Not for establishing a record. Its only purpose for you is getting a warning. And the warning requires one thing: you admit a small human error, and you mean it.

The famous question comes: "Do you know why I stopped you?" And the answer is:

"Officer, I was driving over the limit and I earned this ticket and you have every reason to issue it. I'm sorry for taking up your time.

In fact, I often make this admission before he even gets a word out. That's called flipping the script. It's respectful. It's honest. It doesn't hand him a specific number. It removes the fight he walked up braced for before he even has an opportunity to ask. The officer isn't your enemy — he's the guy holding the opening offer. A person who admits a their error up front and *apologizes* for taking up the cop's time is someone he can let off with a warning and feel good about it. Remember this, if you are going to apologize don't just be sorry, be sorry for something affecting the officer. His time, the need for him to come after you, for him getting wet in the rain. It's much more sincere and less self-serving

Admit — Without Making a Speech

Admit the human situation, not a precise speed or a legal conclusion. You can acknowledge the officer's concern without blurting, 'I did it! I did it!' Be candid, brief, and respectful. Don't invent excuses, and don't argue at the window.

Mitigate

Once you've de-escalated and acknowledged the situation, mitigate. Offer one brief, truthful reason to consider a warning. If a citation seems inevitable, politely ask whether a lesser, non-point violation is available. That's the curbside plea bargain. Make the request once, then stop talking.

If the Ticket Is Coming Anyway — The One Question You Must Ask

Sometimes you run the D-A-M-N System perfectly and still get a ticket. NOW means you take the opportunity to seek a warning or reduction before the ticket is written, not months later after fines and insurance consequences begin. If the officer declines, accept the answer calmly and preserve your options.

When it happens, accept the ticket gracefully. Don't argue. Don't sulk. The roadside conversation is over, and everything you say from this point forward is either neutral or harmful. Except for one question. And you must ask it every single time a ticket lands in your hand.

"Officer, am I allowed to plead guilty by mail on this?" Calm. Polite. No edge in it. Just a cooperative person trying to understand his options. Here's what that question does. The moment you ask it, the officer thinks you're going to mail it in and plead guilty. Which means there's no reason to write extensive notes on the stop. No reason to prepare testimony. No reason to block out a morning in court waiting to testify against you. So, he almost always skips it. He moves on, jots the basics, and that's his preparation.

One question, asked politely, every time a ticket is received. It costs you nothing. It can buy you everything. Don't leave the roadside without asking it.

On your rights: D-A-M-N is a strategy for the ordinary speeding stop where cooperation serves you. You're never required to answer questions beyond the stop, you can decline searches, and if things escalate you have the right to stay quiet and ask whether you're free to go. Cooperation and your constitutional rights aren't opposites — know both and use judgment about which the moment calls for.

The Mail, the Plea, and the Magic of No Notes

Now we leave the roadside and get into the paperwork — and the single most underrated question in this field: What happens to the officer's memory between the day he writes your ticket and the day your case is resolved? Master that question and you've found the soft underbelly of the whole system.

Why the notes are everything

At trial, a traffic case rests almost entirely on one witness: the cop. And months after a routine unmemorable stop, he won't have any recollection of you whatsoever. You were one of hundreds. What he remembers is what he wrote down. If those notes are thorough, his testimony is bulletproof. If they're sparse or missing, a skeptical judge can find reasonable doubt. And a driver who's clearly going to plead guilty by mail gives the officer no reason to prepare, keep careful notes, or show up at all. (Whether you can dispose of a case by mail depends on your jurisdiction — check yours before assuming anything.)

The plea-by-mail move people misread

A written not guilty plea in some courts can travel with a polite letter asking for a reduction, driving school, or no points — a quiet negotiation conducted entirely on paper, no courtroom, no officer present. In places that allow trial by declaration, the officer has to submit his response in writing too — and if he misses the deadline, some systems dismiss. You just created a deadline he has to hit, from your kitchen table.

The chef's kiss: Find exactly what your court allows by mail and choose the route that gives the officer the least reason to prepare and the judge the easiest reason to be kind. Confirm the rules before you mail anything, because a wrong assumption can waive a right you wanted to keep.

Professional Courtesy — PBA Cards and the Art of Being Known

This is the chapter most traffic books are afraid to write. Since this isn't most traffic books, I want to be very clear upfront about what I'm not doing here. I'm not telling you to obtain anything by questionable means. I'm not telling you to misrepresent yourself to a law enforcement officer. I'm not telling you to do anything that could get you into more trouble than a speeding ticket. What I am telling you is about a phenomenon that has existed in American traffic enforcement long before I started driving, and that any honest guide has a duty to mention.

What a PBA card is

Police benevolent associations are the unions and fraternal organizations of law enforcement. Officers who are members can, in many departments, obtain courtesy cards — sometimes called PBA cards — that they give to family members, close friends, and people who have done genuine service to their community. When someone is pulled over and produces one, it signals a connection to the law enforcement community.

Officers are not required to honor them. Some do; some don't. Eagan couldn't have cared less. It varies by department, by officer, by mood, by the seriousness of the stop, and by whether the person presenting it is behaving like a calm human being or like an idiot. A PBA card in the hands of someone who has just screamed at a cop for three minutes is worth exactly nothing. In the hands of someone who has already executed the D-A-M-N chapter perfectly and genuinely has a connection to law enforcement; it can sometimes be the difference between a warning and a ticket.

Thank-you letters and genuine relationships

Here's the piece of this that requires no card and no connection and no anything. When a police department, a precinct, or an individual officer does something commendable in your community — you can write a letter. A real letter. To the chief, to the department, to the officer's commanding officer. Not asking for anything. Not fishing. Just a genuine, specific, thoughtful acknowledgment that you noticed something good.

People in law enforcement are accustomed to getting complaints. A letter of genuine appreciation is genuinely rare, and it builds the kind of goodwill that isn't transactional — it's just what decent people do, and it has a way of coming back around in forms you don't plan for.

Police charity — the clean version

Benevolent associations, widows and orphans' funds, youth programs, and similar initiatives run by police departments are legitimate charities that do legitimate good. Donating to them because you believe in what they do is a perfectly normal thing. It builds community. It supports families of fallen officers. It funds programs that actually help cops and their families.

It does not and should not be understood as a guarantee of anything. Officers aren't for sale, and if you think of a charity donation primarily as a bribe, you've misunderstood both the donation and the officer. People who approach this transactionally usually end up embarrassing themselves. Do it because it's right. Whatever else follows is between you and the universe.

The honest bottom line: Professional courtesy exists. It's been part of American traffic enforcement for generations. The factors that make it work — genuine human connection, respectful behavior, a real relationship with the law enforcement community — are the same factors that make every other strategy in this book work. None of it is magic, and none of it works in the hands of someone who has already violated the first principle: treat the officer like a human being doing a job, not an obstacle between you and your destination.

What Doesn't Work — A Field Guide to Self-Destruction

I've spent this entire book telling you what to do. Let's spend a chapter on what not to do, because the disaster stories are both more entertaining and — for some readers — more instructive than the success stories. I've watched every one of these fail, many of them in my own courtroom.

Arguing

The most reliable path to a ticket in the history of traffic enforcement is arguing with the officer at the window. I don't mean politely clarifying. I mean the full performance: raised voice, constitutional lecture, demands to see the radar certificate, exasperated sighs, and the classic "Do you know who I am?"

The moment you argue, you've done two things. You've taken away the officer's easiest out — the warning he was maybe already thinking about — and you've made the ticket a matter of professional dignity. Now it's not just policy. Now it's personal. He was professionally challenged by a civilian at the window of his cruiser and writing you up is the response that restores order. You didn't just earn the ticket; you made it inevitable.

If arguing worked even a small percentage of the time, I'd tell you. It doesn't. I've never seen it work in thirty-five years. Not once. The drivers who argue get the ticket, get the surly interaction, and often get the maximum fine. The drivers who are boring and polite often get off with a warning. That's the data.

The Golden Beach Incident

We return to Firestarter Nat the World War II Hump Pilot. He survived icing, storms, mountains, mechanical failures, and Japanese fighters. After experiences like that, he developed a complicated relationship with authority. Looking back, I suspect part of it was the military. During the war he spent years taking orders from *superior* officers who thoughtlessly sent him out into pointless life-and-death missions. After the war, he developed a highly tuned sense of contempt for authority that wore a uniform, perhaps born of a lingering undiagnosed case of PTSD.

He refused to be told what to do. Especially by a twenty-five-year-old police officer. One evening he and my brother were driving through Golden Beach, Florida. Golden Beach is a tiny high-income municipality located right on the Miami-Dade and Broward County line. For decades it had a reputation as one of South Florida's premier speed traps.

According to my brother's eyewitness account, and he's the historian of this event, my father was doing approximately sixty-five miles per hour in a 30 mile per hour zone. In Golden Beach, that was ambitious, perhaps even a flagrant disregard of the law.

The lights came on. Everything that should have happened next didn't. The officer approached the car and my father immediately decided that cooperation was overrated. The discussion quickly became an argument. The argument became a confrontation. The confrontation became a shouting match. My brother was trying to calm him down. The officer was trying to control the stop. My father was trying to win an unwinnable debate. If you can't do the time, don't do the crime.

Eventually the situation deteriorated to the point where the officer instructed him to follow the patrol car back to the station. Most people, upon arriving at the station, recognize that the negotiation has ended. Not Firestarter Nat. The shouting continued. The desk sergeant became involved. The volume increased. At some point my father looked directly at the officer and asked: "Have you been drinking?" This did not improve matters much as Nat had probably correctly diagnosed the problem. According to my brother, the officer immediately started moving toward my father while the sergeant physically restrained him and turned to my brother.

"You better get him out of here." Words you never want to hear from a police sergeant. The final score: one speeding ticket, license confiscated, two points transferred back to New Jersey. And absolutely nothing gained.

The most painful part came later. Prior to the ticket, my father was carrying eight points on his New Jersey license. Those two

Golden Beach points brought him up to 10. Twelve points triggered a mandatory suspension. He was one ticket away. That DMV notice sat on his bathroom mirror where he saw it every morning before driving to work. For months, maybe years. A daily reminder of a completely futile confrontation with zero upside.

Here's the recovering attorney lesson issued from the comfort of my armchair. The officer had already won the moment the lights came on. The question was never whether my father could defeat the officer in a roadside debate. The question was whether he could minimize the damage. Instead, he escalated. He argued. He challenged authority. He made it personal. He turned a routine traffic stop into a contest of wills. And contests of will with armed government employees never end well.

Today I teach De-escalate. Admit. Mitigate. NOW!

Firestarter Nat's experience taught the opposite lesson. Argue. Escalate. Aggravate. And then pay for it. The irony is that my father was one of the most aware drivers I've ever known. He could spot a speed trap a mile away. He understood traffic patterns instinctively. He drove hundreds of thousands of miles with remarkably few accidents. But awareness behind the wheel doesn't help much once the lights are flashing in your mirror. At that point, the game changes. The roadside is no longer about speed. It's about psychology. And Golden Beach taught me exactly how not to play that game.

The Sovereign Citizen Approach

Every few years, the internet rediscovers the sovereign citizen theory: the idea that by invoking certain magic phrases and sections from the Declaration of Independence, you become exempt from all vehicle traffic and safety laws. He might even produce a particular document in support of that position. I want to be completely unambiguous about this.

The sovereign citizen argument has never, not once, in the entire documented history of American traffic court, worked. Not one time. Officers are now trained specifically to handle these encounters, and the training amounts to stay calm, write the ticket, and move on. Judges have seen it so many times that sovereign citizen arguments can actually make a case worse, because you've now signaled to the court that you're not a reasonable person who made a small mistake — you're a disruptor with a philosophy. That's a much harder sell when you're asking for a conditional discharge. If you're currently developing a sovereign citizen strategy for your ticket, my candid advice is don't bother.

Fake emergencies

The fake emergency is a time-honored tradition that fails at a consistent and impressive rate, because officers have heard every emergency ever invented and have gotten quite good at evaluating whether they sound real.

The structural problem with any story that depends on an unverifiable claim is that it might become verifiable in the next thirty seconds, and officers with smartphones and radios have a lot of ways to verify things. Which brings me back to my story of my *sick* son. And you already know how that one worked out.

Lesson: never tell a lie that can be verified in thirty seconds. And if your mitigation story depends on another witness, make sure the witness knows he's a witness. Better yet just tell the truth and keep it short.

The dumbest defense I ever watched

I've been in a lot of courtrooms over a long career, and I've watched a lot of people defend speeding tickets in ways that ranged from uninspired to genuinely inadvisable. But this one lives in its own category.

A driver — not my client, just someone I was watching from the gallery — stood up and told the judge, with complete confidence, that his car's speedometer was broken. Plausible enough so far. Then the officer on the stand, who had clearly been waiting for exactly this, produced the citation notes and read aloud the make, model, year, and mileage of the vehicle: a ten-year-old sedan with over 180,000 miles.

Then the officer said, pleasantly: "Your Honor, I followed this vehicle for approximately half a mile and paced it at 73 miles per hour, and the driver admitted such according to my notes. The vehicle appeared to be operating normally in all other respects."

The driver's attorney — and God bless him, he tried — stood up and said his client maintained the speedometer was defective. The judge looked at the driver and said, with the weary patience of a man who has been doing this for twenty years: "Sir, how did you know what speed you were going?" Long pause. Convicted. Next.

What all the failures have in common

Every approach that doesn't work shares one feature: it creates friction. It makes the officer's job harder. It gives the prosecutor something to fight. It makes the judge's morning worse. Everything in the successful half of this book does the opposite — it makes you the easiest, least complicated, most pleasant file on the docket. Be the easy yes. It is, by a wide margin, the most effective legal strategy available to a non-lawyer, and most lawyers use it too.

PART IV
BEATING THE SYSTEM

The Lawyer's Thirty-Five-Year Strategy

This is the chapter people bought the book for and I will earn it. Thirty-five years after reading Trooper Eagan's book, I still don't have a magic word. I have a posture and a sequence, sharpened over a career, and a personal record that says it works: seven stops in fourteen Florida years, five warnings, two conditional discharges — one settled at the curb before the officer's pen was dry.

Talking your way out, honestly

This isn't con artistry. It's the D-A-M-N chapter applied: admit the error of your ways, de-escalate all the way down, one honest mitigating reason, then stop talking. It works more than two-thirds of the time not because of charm, but because I never give the officer the fight he expected, thus depriving him of a reason to dig in.

The curbside plea bargain

When an officer has decided he's writing something, there's sometimes room — respectfully, never demanding — to ask whether he might write it for a lesser charge. "Officer, I understand. Is there any way to write this so it doesn't put points on my license? I'd really appreciate it." No pressure. Accept whatever answer comes. Asked politely, this costs nothing and occasionally hands you a citation that's half-beaten before you see a courthouse. Two of my stops ended exactly this way.

When to hire a professional

The flip side of thirty-five years is knowing when to get out of your own way. Get a traffic lawyer when the charge crosses into criminal territory. When a conviction would suspend a license you can't afford to lose. When it's a commercial license. When you're charged far from home and can't keep appearing. A few hundred dollars to a lawyer who works that courthouse every week, knows the prosecutor, knows which judge deals — measured against a multi-thousand-dollar insurance surcharge — isn't a cost. It's the single best trade in this book.

And here's a secret about small towns and cities. There's often one attorney that knows the judge, the clerk and every cop in town, or as I call him the *Town Fixer*. They are not always easy to identify as that term is not on their business card or LinkedIn profile. But they exist. There are several ways to identify them. First, call the clerk and ask I have a ticket and need representation. Can you tell me a few good attorneys that appear in your court regularly? That might work. Next, go to the court before your appearance date and watch the action. Get their early because the fixer's cases are definitely going to be called first; after all that's why he's the fixer. Finally, if you have some political contacts ask them, they all know.

My Personal Experience

In New York State, 3 speeding tickets within 18 months equals automatic revocation. I had two tickets I was unable to beat using the above strategies. Both from local cops who had a habit of showing up in court at the worst possible moment. I got my 3rd ticket from the trooper who I tried to lie my way out of, stating my son was ill. And you'll see how that worked out. So, I called my friend, the councilman and asked him who to hire. He gave me a name. I hired him on the spot.

We go to court at 8:15 am. The judge walks in and nods at my attorney. Judge makes an announcement that those defendants appearing with an attorney would be called first and then quickly called again. No cop and the case is dismissed. Guess whose case got called first? No trooper. Then the judge takes another case, rushes through it at the speed that judges aren't supposed to go. He then calls my case again, two minutes later and still no trooper. Case dismissed and we run out of the courtroom because if the trooper showed up, it was all over for me.

How to Talk to a Judge

If you end up standing in front of a judge, let me save you from yourself. I've watched a thousand people torch a winnable case in the first ten seconds just by being exactly who they are. A judge is not your buddy, your therapist, or your audience. A judge is a tired, smart, deeply skeptical human being who has heard every excuse ever invented, twice, before lunch. Your whole job is to be the one refreshing exception in a long gray morning of excuses.

Three things a judge actually wants

- Respect. 'Yes, Your Honor.' 'Thank you, Your Honor.' Stand when you speak. Don't interrupt. The robe isn't about the person; it's about the institution and understanding that difference marks you immediately as someone who belongs in the room.
- Brevity. Make your point and stop. The fastest way to lose a judge is to ramble. The litigant who says one clear thing and sits down is a gift. The one who delivers a ten-minute monologue about how unfair everything is gets a conviction to free up the docket.

- Credibility. It's the whole game.

Credibility is the only currency

You have exactly one asset in that room: whether the judge believes you. Don't lie. Don't exaggerate. Don't pile up four excuses in a row — it's a lost cause. One honest, specific, reasonable point lands a hundred times harder than a full defense that's half-fabricated. The moment a judge catches you stretching the truth, everything else you say turns to vapor.

One fight at a time. Walk in with your single strongest point, concede whatever isn't worth fighting, and let your reasonableness carry the weight.

Dress like you respect the room

No one's asking for a tuxedo. But show up looking like you took the morning seriously — a collar, clean clothes, like you're meeting someone who matters. Because you are. The judge clocks it the second you walk in. It answers a question already forming in their mind: is this a serious person, or a problem? Dress the answer before you open your mouth.

The secret: judges deal with angry, unprepared, self-pitying people all day. When somebody walks in respectful, well-dressed, prepared, brief, honest, and with one small reasonable ask — the judge is genuinely relieved. And relieved judges are generous judges. Be the easy yes. It works at the window, it works with the prosecutor, and it works — maybe most of all — on the person in the robe.

The Courtroom — Adjourn, Adjourn, Adjourn

If you've decided to fight, and after reading this book you had better, then understand this lesson; the courtroom is a game of attrition, and time is your indispensable ally. Here's the brutal truth first, then the leverage.

There's really only one guaranteed way to win

Let me give it to you straight. In the thirty-five years since reading Trooper Eagan's book, I know exactly what my record shows: I've beaten tickets by an officer no-show at least ten times. As mentioned before, I have never won a ticket at a contested hearing, despite my training; not once. I've only had two live hearings. I learned early on that the hearing is to be avoided, not won. That's coming from a lawyer trained for this.

The goal isn't to out-argue the officer. The goal is to outlast him. If the officer shows up with clean notes, calibrated equipment, and a clear account of the stop — you're going to be convicted. You could be Clarence Darrow reincarnated and your chances are between slim to none. Recognize a losing hand and pivot to a plea, a reduction, or driving school before you waste everybody's morning, especially your own.

Who shows up — and who doesn't

Not every officer no-shows at the same rate and understanding geography is key. A local cop in a small town will almost always show up. He works in that town, the courthouse is around the corner, and if he starts blowing off court dates, the chief will hear about it. Accountability is tight.

In bigger cities, more volume means less accountability. The odds of a no-show tick up. But the real gift is the state trooper. Troopers cover enormous geographic areas across multiple towns. They often live far from where they patrol. They get transferred, promoted, go out on sick leave, or retire. A trooper has a dozen acceptable reasons to not be in your specific courtroom on your specific morning six months after writing the ticket. For damn near every one of my no-show wins, that's the math that did it. If a trooper wrote your ticket, time can be your best friend.

The leverage: it all rests on one witness

- The no-show: state usually has no case, most courts dismiss. Officers are human — they move, they transfer, they have conflicts.
- The two-officer stop: where one clocked you and another wrote the ticket, the state needs both. If the one who clocked you doesn't appear, the chain breaks.

- Thin notes: an officer testifying from sparse memory months later is an officer whose certainty a skeptical judge may chip away at.
- Equipment foundation: radar and laser depend on proper calibration and regular testing along with a trained operator and records that prove it. If the state can't establish this, the case may not be proven. Technical — this is where a lawyer earns the fee.

Why time is your ally

Every legitimate continuance is one more date the officer has to keep clear. One more chance for a transfer, retirement, promotion, or conflict to intervene. One more stretch of time erasing his memory of a stop he never really remembered anyway. Heck he might even be out catching bad guys. You never know.

Plead not guilty. Request the hearing. When the system offers a chance to reset the date — take it. Adjourn, adjourn, adjourn — until you're finally forced to appear.

Courts grant adjournments readily when you have a legitimate reason on paper. A plane ticket showing you'll be out of town. Proof of a work commitment, a medical appointment, a documented real conflict. Keep every request legitimate and documented and you can stretch the calendar a long way — often far enough for a trooper's life to move him right off your case.

Two hard cautions: never lie to a court and never file a frivolous request — that's far worse trouble than a speeding ticket. And never miss your own court date. A default conviction, extra fees, even a suspension or a warrant can follow. Adjourn means properly requesting a new date. Appear every single time, until the case is done.

The Strategic Delay: Running Out the Clock on Your Points

Here's the advanced version of the adjourn strategy, and one of the most underappreciated moves in the whole playbook.

Most states run on a rolling window for points — usually 12, 24, or 36 months depending on the jurisdiction. When points hit your record, they generally relate back to the date the ticket was issued, not when you were convicted. Which means that if you delay the final court disposition long enough, your oldest points may have expired and already dropped off your active record, well before the new ticket's points ever officially land.

Think about what that means if you're sitting on the edge of a suspension. Say your state has a 12-point limit and you're carrying 9. You're one bad conviction away from losing your license. The instinct is to fight to prove your innocence. But that's often the wrong fight. The right fight is the calendar.

Here's the clock math. You receive the ticket. You plead not guilty. You begin requesting adjournments with legitimate documented reasons — a business trip, a medical appointment, a scheduling conflict. Six months pass. Nine months. The clock on your oldest points is running the whole time. If those old points were from an incident 18 months ago and your window is 24 months, you're getting close. Delay the case past that expiration date and those old points die — quietly, automatically, with no hearing required.

Now comes the key: the system evaluates your driving record at the moment of conviction, not the moment of the violation. So, when you finally walk into that courtroom — even if you plead guilty to the charge on the table — the points that would have pushed you over the cliff are already gone. You pay the fine. You take the new points. But the old points that would have triggered the suspension are dead, and your license survives.

The timeline: old points active, license at risk → ticket received → adjourn, adjourn, adjourn → old points expire, the safe zone → plea or conviction → license saved.

You didn't prove your innocence. You didn't beat the officer on cross. You just understood how the clock works and let it run. That is a completely legitimate use of the legal process, and it saves licenses that would otherwise be lost.

One further tactic. Let's say you've gotten the maximum adjournments and you're still a few weeks away from point expiration, what should you do? At that point it's time to hire an attorney and let him get and adjournment. Assuming you've hired someone well know to the court, he'll likely be able to adjourn you at least one more time and perhaps even more.

One warning: this only works when you use legitimate adjournments — never when you blow off a court date. As previously stated, Failure to Appear triggers its own suspension and a bench warrant that lights you up on every database in the country.

The delay has to be legal, documented, and court-approved every step of the way. Play it right and the calendar is your best lawyer.

When to Fold — Driving School and the Conditional Discharge

A lot of this book is about fighting. This chapter is about knowing when to stop fighting and take a good deal — because the goal was never to win the argument. The goal was always to protect the license and keep your insurance premiums from exploding.

Driving school: the most underrated move in the book

In Florida and many other states, electing a driver-improvement course keeps points off your record, frequently even when you just pay the fine. Now you take the course online. You give up an afternoon and a small course fee. The conviction never reaches your insurer as points. Your record stays clean.

For a first ticket where the officer clearly has you dead to rights, this is almost always the correct call. You're not surrendering. You're trading a few hours for the multi-year insurance surcharge you'd otherwise eat. That's not folding. That's winning quietly, which is the best way to win.

- Eligibility is usually limited — once every twelve or eighteen months. Don't burn it on a ticket you could have beaten outright.
- Confirm with the court that finishing the course actually keeps the points off before you elect it. Ask the clerk directly.
- Some states bundle school with a deferral, so the charge disappears on completion. Always ask if that's available.

The conditional discharge: the beautiful outcome

Both of my Florida tickets ended here, and it's a magnificent result when you can get it. The court holds the charge in abeyance: stay clean for a set period and the charge gets dismissed or never reported as a conviction. No points, no surcharge, nothing on the record.

It's often available on first offenses for drivers with clean histories. Which is, again, why keeping your record clean is its own long-term strategy. A spotless history is the currency that buys mercy on the day you need it.

My first time, after 7 years of living in Florida, the judge actually complimented me on my exemplary driving record. I almost laughed at the thought, but I was thankful that New York and Florida didn't talk much. You can't make this stuff up.

And even better, it says on the front of my license in red ink **Safe Driver**. In Florida, maintaining a spotless record for three consecutive years—free of points, at-fault accidents, or suspensions—earns you an official **Safe Driver** designation on your license and can lower insurance premiums.

The whole book in one paragraph

Drive awake. Never pass a moving trooper. Run a legal detector and a good app. Know what a conviction truly costs before you decide whether to fight it. Know the rules of the specific state you're in. If you get stopped: De-escalate, Admit, Mitigate, NOW!, then stop talking. Use the mail and the calendar as the tools they are. Talk to a judge with respect, brevity, and credibility. Fight only where you've got real leverage — one issue at a time. And when the deal in front of you protects your license and your insurance premium: take it, thank the man, and drive home at the limit.

My Greatest Hits

Alright. Enough strategy. Let me tell you some stories, because the lessons live in the stories better than they ever live in a list. Thirty-five years of stops, courts, prosecutors, and judges — some of which I won, some of which I didn't, and all of which taught me something. The original book was often a life/license saver.

(Fair warning: the one I lost is in this chapter too. It belongs here for the same reason the wins do — because losing honestly is more instructive than winning vaguely.)

The Hot Date in Jupiter

As I mentioned earlier, this was the Jupiter stop — 64 in a 45, three blown stop signs, and instead of arguing I told the young cop he had to write me up because I'd earned it. It broke his software completely. But the part I left out before is what happened next.

He actually said: "Wait a minute. What's going on here?"

Then he asked why I was in such a hurry. I told him the truth. "I'm late for a date."

He asked: "Is she hot?"

I said: "Smoking."

He laughed. We chatted for another minute. And I drove away with no ticket.

Almost one year from that date Tiger Woods was arrested in the same exact spot by the same cop.

Here's why that worked for me and not Tiger, and it wasn't the date: it worked because I didn't argue. I didn't make him defend himself. I admitted I screwed up, lowered the temperature, and gave him a reason to smile. That's the entire D-A-M-N chapter performed live on the shoulder of a Florida road. He expected denial, excuses, anger — and the second he didn't get any of it, the ticket stopped being automatic. And I wasn't driving under the influence.

The Curbside Save

My favorite, because it never even made it to a courthouse.

He walks up, asks the famous question, "Do you know why I stopped you?" And I give him the famous answer: "Officer, I think I wasn't paying attention to my speed and it got away from me. I'm sorry you have to spend your time on this." No fight, no number, no speech. He relaxes about half a notch. And right there, before the pen touches the pad, I ask the quiet question: "Is there any way to write this so it doesn't put points on my license? I'd really appreciate it."

He looks at me; he looks down at his pad. Then he writes me for a non-moving violation. Case closed at the curb. No points, no court, no surcharge. The whole war over before it started, because I gave him an easy yes instead of a hard fight. That's the entire book in ninety seconds on the shoulder of a Florida road.

The Five Warnings

Five of my seven Florida stops never became tickets at all. The secret is the same every single time: I was boring. Polite. I owned the mistake, kept it short, and shut up and let the officer decide. The drivers who get the ticket are almost always the ones who argued, lied, performed, or talked until the cop figured the paperwork was easier than the conversation. I just refused to be that driver. Four times out of six, the warning was the path of least resistance — for him as much as for me.

The First Ticket I Ever Beat

Long before I was a lawyer, before I knew the first thing about courtrooms or radar or adjournment strategy, I beat a speeding ticket almost entirely by accident. I'd pleaded not guilty mostly out of stubbornness, legitimately adjourned it 3 times and showed up at an upstate New York Justice Court on a cold Tuesday morning. I found myself in a room with forty other people all awaiting a similar fate. I was twenty-something, nervous, and clueless.

My case got called. I stood up. The officer wasn't there. The judge looked at the calendar, looked at the empty prosecution table, looked at me, and said something along the lines of: "Case dismissed for failure to prosecute, sir you're free to go."

I walked out into the parking lot, stood in the cold for a minute, and had what I can only describe as an epiphany. It was something they never taught me in law school. I hadn't done anything clever. I hadn't argued or strategized or cross-examined. I just showed up. The officer didn't. And the entire machinery of traffic enforcement, which had seemed so inevitable and imposing one moment, glitched and moved on to the next file.

That morning Woody Allen's immortal words came back to me. "80 percent of life is showing up." And adjourning to the max meant I had a pretty fair chance of winning, because when the cop fails to appear, you've almost always won. That's where my speeding ticket strategy was born.

The No-Show Morning I'll Never Forget

I've beaten no-shows at least ten times over the years, but this one stands out. Trooper case, upstate New York highway. I'd gotten the ticket on a Friday afternoon from a trooper who covered a large stretch of the Thruway. I pleaded not guilty, requested a hearing, and then started working the calendar. First date: I had a plane ticket. Adjournment granted. Second date: documented work commitment. Adjournment granted. Third date: I appeared in court. Looked around the room. Waited.

The trooper's name got called. Silence. Called again. More silence. The court officer spoke quietly to the prosecutor. The prosecutor shuffled some papers. The judge looked up and said, with the practiced brevity of someone who has been doing this a long time: "Case dismissed. Officer failed to appear. Next."

The whole thing took about four minutes from time my name was called to me walking out the door. Four minutes and three adjournments, and the Thruway Patrol's scheduling problem became my pathway to acquittal. I later found out that the trooper had been promoted and transferred six weeks earlier. The promotion came with the freedom to avoid court unless absolutely necessary. Nobody had bothered to notify the court.

That's the geography lesson in action. A local cop would've been around the corner. The trooper had moved his entire life to a different county.

The Honor Student on the Taconic

My stepson got a ticket on the Taconic Parkway: 80 in a 55. Not a love tap. We plead not guilty and appear. The courtroom is jammed. Before anyone's called, the prosecutor announces to the room: there will be no plea bargaining from a moving violation to a non-moving violation. Period. I'm already recalculating, figuring we knock 80 down to 59 in a 55 and save the worst of the points.

Then we get up to the prosecutor. I hand him my attorney card. I explain, quietly, that my stepson is an honor student who needs to keep a clean driving record. He pleaded it down to illegal parking.

Illegal parking. On the Taconic Parkway. From 80 in a 55. The exact reduction he'd told the entire room he wouldn't give. Because sometimes lawyers do get a better deal than you can get for yourself and sometimes pronouncements like that are really offers in disguise.

Then I had a little fun with the kid. I told him I'd happily pay the fine, but his mother was going to be furious with me about the whole episode, so the ticket was on him. He was happy to pay, as he should have been.

Two lessons: first, in courts that allow plea bargaining — and most of upstate New York and many other states do — a lawyer will almost always get you more than you'll get on your own, because he knows the room. Second, "no plea bargaining" announced to a crowd is an opening offer. It always has been. You know where you've heard that before.

The Smartest Move I Ever Watched

This one wasn't mine. I was watching from the gallery at a courthouse I had business in. A driver representing himself caught my full attention. The officer took the stand and gave his testimony: he had clocked the defendant at 79 miles per hour in a 55-zone using a properly calibrated laser unit.

The driver, a quiet man in a decent suit who had clearly done his homework, asked the officer one question on cross: "Officer, when was the laser unit in your possession last calibrated by a certified technician, and do you have the documentation with you today?"

The officer looked at the prosecutor. The prosecutor looked at the officer. Neither of them had the documentation. The judge dismissed.

The driver had gone to the police department ahead of time, made a public records request for the calibration logs, discovered they were overdue, and built his entire case around one clean technical question. One question, asked calmly, in the right sequence, by a man who had done his homework and wasn't swinging at everything. One fight at a time. I almost applauded from the gallery.

The Lesson Under All of It

Read these stories and you might think sure, but he's a lawyer. He knows things I don't. Some of that's true, but almost none of what saved me was law. It was behavior. It was understanding that every person in that chain, from the cop to the clerk to the judge, is a tired human being looking for the easy path — and deciding, on purpose, to be that easy path for them. You don't need a law degree for that. You need to read the room, keep your mouth disciplined, and remember the sentence we started with:

It's not a verdict. It's an opening offer presented to you by a man in Raybans standing by your car saying, "Boy, you're in a heap of trouble." Every story in this book is just me, refusing to accept the opening offer and it should be you too.

PART V
THE FUTURE

Bonus:

The Future of Traffic Enforcement

Let me put on my Financial Survival Network hat for a minute, because this game is about to change — and the smart money reads the trend before the trend reads them.

The car starts driving itself

I drive a Tesla and run Full Self-Driving hard. And here's the thing nobody quite wants to say: a car that drives itself doesn't speed the way you do. It holds a set speed, reads the signs, and doesn't get antsy behind a trooper doing sixty-five. As more of the fleet goes semi-autonomous, a whole category of human speeding behavior starts to disappear. That's good for safety. It's complicated for an enforcement system that has come to depend on the revenue.

Enforcement goes automated too

Watch what they do, not what they say. As human officers get more expensive and human speeding gets rarer, enforcement leans harder on automation — speed cameras, average-speed corridors, AI-driven systems that flag a violation with no human in the loop. The ticket already arrives in your mailbox with a photo. The next step is a seamless automated pipeline, and there's no window to charm your way through.

- Bad news: you can't talk your way out of a camera. The entire human strategy of this book does nothing against a machine.
- Good news: machines make mistakes and machines create records. Every automated system is only as good as its calibration, its signage, its maintenance logs — all of which are paper trails you or your lawyer can demand and challenge. The fight just moves from the officer's memory to the machine's documentation.

My read: fewer human stops, more automated ones. The high-leverage moment at the window becomes rarer and more precious. The technical documentary fight over machine evidence becomes more important. Enjoy the D-A-M-N era while it lasts. The next edition of this book will have a lot more to say about fighting robots.

Drive Smart. Drive Awake.

In thirty-five years, since reading Trooper Eagan's magnum opus, I learned one thing: Most tickets are won or lost before the officer reaches your window. Stay calm. Be respectful. Never pass a moving trooper. Know what you're really fighting — not a $250 fine, but a $2,500 five-year tax. Give the officer, the prosecutor, and the judge a reason to be kind. Use the calendar. Take the deal when the deal is good. And remember the sentence that opened this book, because it's the sentence that closes it:

A speeding ticket isn't a verdict. It's the opening offer delivered by an armed agent in Raybans. You can't reject the ticket but you are free to reject the offer.

Seven stops. Five warnings. Two cured. Not luck. A system. Now that system is yours.

THE AUDIO UPGRADE

For a small upgrade, grab the full audio companion — a deep-dive podcast edition of every chapter. The whole book reborn as a conversation, built for the road, so you can absorb the entire strategy hands-free between the speed trap at the bottom of the hill and your own driveway.

Same hard-won material. New format. Perfect for the windshield time where, let's be honest, you were going to need it anyway.

Scan to listen · bit.ly/Speeders_Audio

— Kerry Lutz

America's Top Recovering Attorney/Alleged Habitual Speeder

The Ten Commandments of the Habitual Speeder

1. Thou Shalt Never Pass a Moving Trooper.
2. Thou Shalt Not Speed in Residential Neighborhoods.
3. Thou Shalt Drive with the Pack.
4. Thou Shalt De-escalate, Admit, Mitigate, and act NOW!.
5. Thou Shalt Never Argue at the Window.
6. Thou Shalt Ask About Pleading Guilty By Mail.
7. Thou Shalt Become the Easy File.
8. Thou Shalt Respect the Calendar.
9. Thou Shalt Protect Thy Insurance Premium.
10. Thou Shalt Remember That a Ticket Is Not a Verdict.

The Speeder's Serenity Prayer

God grant me the serenity to accept the speed traps I cannot avoid,

The courage to fight the tickets that can be beaten,

And the wisdom to know the difference.

Keep me from passing moving troopers,

Protect me from instant-on radar and my own stupidity,

Help me to drive with the pack,

And remind me that insurance surcharges are forever.

May my detector be quiet,

My Waze reports accurate,

My judge merciful,

And my driving record forever exemplary.

And if I should fail in these endeavors,

Grant me a conditional discharge and no points.

Amen.

Firestarter Nat's Final Rule

"It's not about speed. It's about awareness."
— Nat Lutz

Hump Pilot • Builder • Early Super Speeder

About the Author

Kerry Lutz is America's Top Recovering Attorney and the founder of the Financial Survival Network. Over more than fifty years of driving and thirty-five years of applying the principles of James Eagan, he has accumulated over one hundred traffic stops, countless courtroom appearances, and enough stories to fill a glove compartment.

Acknowledgments

To James M. Eagan, whose classic book inspired generations of drivers. And to Firestarter Nat, who taught me that awareness beats horsepower.

If this book has helped you — or if you believe it could help someone you know — please leave a review wherever you purchased it. Every review helps us reach more drivers who need this information. Their licenses, their insurance premiums, and their driving records may be hanging in the balance. A thirty-second review from you could save someone years of consequences. Thank you for reading, and drive awake.

---

www.ingramcontent.com/pod-product-compliance
Lightning Source LLC
LaVergne TN
LVHW041208061126
851857LV00018B/1982